A DEDICATORY INSCRIPTION
OF THE URARTIAN KING IŠPUINI

Mirjo Salvini

The silver situla, here edited, is one of the few items of this type
which are well known from the royal Assyrian reliefs connected with
the ceremony of the tree. The inscription is a dedication of the object by the Urartian king Išpuini (ca. 825-810 B.C.) for his grandson
Inušpua who has here the otherwise unknown "title" of *kibāru* (or
kibarru). The language is Assyrian and this is the first case of a non-
monumental inscription of an Urartian king in this language. It is
evident that an Assyrian scribal school existed at the Urartian capital
Tušpa, at least at the time of Sarduri Ist, father of Išpuini, and now
it is also probable that a sort of bilinguialism was present within the
leading class of Urartu. The situla is to be dated around 810 B.C.

The cuneiform inscription edited here is the dedicatory inscription in Assyrian language on a silver situla,
which appeared during 1976 in the antique-trade of Munich. The present whereabouts is unknown, but an
electrogalvanic copy is in the possession of the Prähistorische Staatssammlung of Munich.[1]

The situla (see Fig. 1)[2] is a small, straight-sided bucket, with a flat bottom. A central handle with the
ends in the form of snake-heads is attached to the body by two vertical rings. The rim is rolled outwards
with a second horizontal ridge underneath. On one side, the inscription runs outlined by an incised rect-
angular frame. Apart from the cuneiform signs the surface of the situla is undecorated.

To my knowledge, only two similar objects from Urartu exist, one of which has an Urartian inscription of
Išpuini himself. All of these have possibly the same origin and were traded through Munich.[3]

---

[1]PS inv. 2008. I wish to thank the Director, Dr. Hans-Jörg Kellner, for the kind permission to study the object in question
and to publish the photo. Size of the situla: height 10 cm., diameter 9 cm. The inscription is 13,8 cm. long and 4 mm.
high. The electrogalvanic copy was on display in the exhibition *Urartu. Ein wiederentdeckter Rivale Assyriens, Katalog
der Ausstellung, herausgegeben von Hans-Jörg Kellner, München 8. September bis 5. Dezember 1976* (hereafter quoted as
Katalog Urartu), No. 107 with pl. 10. I also wish to thank Prof. K. Deller for his contribution to the interpretation of
the text.

[2]For the exact definition of "situla" as "Wassergefäss mit Bügelhenkel" see P. Calmeyer, *Reliefbronzen in babylonischem
Stil*, München 1973, p. 133 n. 105 (= BJV 6 1966, p. 60 n. 5). Often objects of a completely different function and
form are definited "situlae": see for instance P. R. S. Moorey, *Catalogue of the Ancient Persian Bronzes in the Ashmolean
Museum*, Oxford 1971, p. 270ff., and L. Vanden Berghe, *Archéologie de l'Irān ancien*, Leiden 1966, p. 91f.
A list of the silver objects from Urartu is to be found by M. N. van Loon, *Urartian Art*, Istanbul 1966, p. 125-28. See
also *Katalog Urartu*, Nos. 223, 224, 228, 229, 234-236.

[3]I plan to publish these pieces together with ontehr inscribed objects in the near future.

Figure 1.

These situlae are very rare objects in the ancient Orient. Outside Urartu I can quote only two more, both in bronze. One, finely decorated, and probably from the area of Ziwiyēh, is in the Metropolitan Museum of New York;[4] the other, undecorated, from Luristān, is preserved in the Ashmolean Museum in Oxford.[5]

Though archaeological objects of this kind are rare, they are frequently represented in Urartian art on bronzes,[6] frescoes,[7] ivories[8] and on cylinder-seal impressions.[9] The most frequent scene, of Assyrian derivation, is the ceremony[10] of the tree with on either side winged genii, each holding a situla in one hand and a "cone" in the other. Situlae are also to be found in the hands of gods, of fantastic beings (šedu) and of human (female?) figures walking in procession.

I give here the transcription and the translation of the text (for the autography see Fig. 2):

[I]*Iš-pu-ú-i-ni* apil(A) [Id]*Sar₅-duri*(BÀD) *ana* (DIŠ) [I]*I-nu-uš-pu-a* ittidini (SUM-*ni*) *ana* (DIŠ) [LÚ]*ki-ba-ri-šú ra-a*ꜣ-*me*
"Išpuini, son of Sarduri, gave (this situla) to Inušpua, to his dear *kibāru/kibarru*."

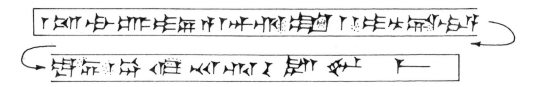

Figure 2.

[4]Ch. K. Wilkinson, "Bulletin of the Metropolitan Museum of Art," Apr. 1963, p. 282, fig. 14, 15.

[5]See Moorey, quoted above n. 2, p. 269, No. 513, fig. 23 and pl. 81.

[6]Cf. B. B. Piotrovskij, *Il regno di Van – Urartu,* Rome 1966, p. 242 and pl. 36, 38; id. *Karmir-Blur, Al'bom,* Leningrad 1970, fig. 44, 45; *Katalog Urartu* fig. 38, 39, 56 and No. 139; *Sotheby's Catalogue of Antiquities and Islamic Art,* 8th December 1975, Nos. 77, 86; O. A. Taşyürek, TAD 21, 1, 1975, p. 177ff., fig. 1. See also the silver pectoral PS inv. 1800, *Katalog Urartu,* No. 236.

[7]T. Özgüç, *Altintepe I,* Ankara 1966, p. 49, pl. I,1; 23,1; K. Oganesjan, *Rospisi Erebuni,* Erevan 1973, pl. 15, 23, 24.

[8]T. Özgüç, *Altintepe II,* Ankara 1969, pl. B (colour), 32, 33.

[9]Cf. I. M. Diakonoff, *Urartskie pis'ma i dokumenty* (= *UPD*), Moscow-Leningrad 1963, pp. 135, 136, 138, 140.

[10]Cf. J. B. Stearns, *Reliefs from the Palace of Ashurnaṣirpal II* (AfO Bh. 15), Graz 1961, p. 25 n. 44, and p. 70. For the typology of situlae represented on Assyrian reliefs cf. B. Hrouda, *Die Kulturgeschichte des assyrischen Flachbildes,* Bonn 1965, p. 77, pl. 19 (Nos. 1-7).

This kind of writing of the name of Sarduri[11] is to be found in the "Sardursburg" inscription at Van Kalesi,[12] in the bilingual stela of Kelišin[13] by Išpuini and Menua (in the Urartian version this writing is found together with the more usual writing $^{Id}Sar_5$-*du-ri*), and in the short Urartian inscription of Išpuini himself on the base of a column found at Aralesk.[14] As far as the phonetic reading of the logogramm BÀD is concerned, for reasons adduced by W. C. Benedict,[15] *duri* is to be preferred to *dur$_8$* (according to AS^2 114).

This syntactic construction seems anomalous in the Neo-assyrian language. On the suggestion of K. Deller, the inscription should be: *Išpuini mar$^?$a Sarduri ana Inušpua* ^{LÚ*}*kibārišu/kibarrišu ra$^?$me ittidini*. Unfortunately no Urartian text offers a parallel for such a construction where the apposition and the name are separated by the verbal predicate.

Despite its brevity, the text allows some interesting suggestions. First of all I would like to point out that this is the first non-monumental inscription of an Urartian king in the Assyrian language. Moreover it is also the first inscription of Išpuini on a metal object.

The only other known Assyrian texts of Urartian kings are those already mentioned above of "Sardursburg" and of Kelišin, and also the Assyrian version of the bilingual stela of Topzawä[16] by Rusa Ist.

The use of the Assyrian language in the Sarduri Ist inscription at Van Kalesi ("Sardursburg"), which is known to be the oldest document from Urartu, is linked to the introduction of cuneiform writing here at the time of the foundation of the Urartian kingdom.

The Assyrian versions of the two bilingual texts can be easily explained through the political relationships between Urartu and the Assyrian Empire. In fact, both the stelae are placed at the southern border of Urartu, namely in contact with the area of Muṣaṣir, which lay under the political and cultural influence of Assyria. We know that prince Urzana of Muṣaṣir used the Assyrian language at the time of Rusa Ist.[17]

The use of the Assyrian language on our situla leads to the conclusion that the school of the Assyrian scribes who introduced the cuneiform writing into Urartu, was still present in the capital Tušpa at the end of Išpuini's reign (see below the date of the situla). This despite the fact that in consequence of reform introduced by Išpuini himself the official language was by that time Urartian. Most probably in Tušpa, and within the leading class, a certain bilingualism was present--for a period at least--and Assyrian was used in court circles.

These considerations make the theory advanced by I. M. Diakonoff,[18] according to which Urartian cuneiform writing is not of direct Neo-assyrian derivation, but rather comes from a Hurrian scribal school of the Mitannian group, highly improbable.

---

[11]Cf. about this J. Friedrich, *Einführung ins Urartäische* (MVAeG 37), Leipzig 1933, p. 22-23.

[12]F. W. König, *Handbuch der chaldischen Inschriften (= HchI)*, AfO Bh. 8, Graz 1955-57, No. 1 a-c; E. Bilgiç, TAD 9 (1969) p. 45ff.

[13]See the edition by W. C. Benedict, *JAOS* 81 (1961) p. 359ff.

[14]*HchI*, No. 5 a.

[15]*Urartian Phonology and Morphology*, diss. Ann Arbor 1958, p. 15 n. 9 and *JAOS* 81 (1961) p. 361.

[16]*HchI*, No. 122.

[17]Cf. F. Thureau-Dangin, *Une relation de la huitième campagne de Sargon (714 av. J.-C.)*, Paris 1912, p. XIff.

[18]*UPD* p. 18, and *Hurrisch und Urartäisch*, München 1971, p. 33 n. 26; but see M. Salvini, *OLZ* 71 (1976) col. 29.

Inušpua, to whom the object is dedicated, was the son of Menua and the grandson of Išpuini.[19] We
know of him from some inscriptions in which his name is associated with that of his grandfather and his
father, or only with that of his father.[20] The inscription of Tabriz Kapisi (HchI 12) at Van Kalesi,
where the three names Išpuini, Menua and Inušpua appear, must be dated towards the end of Išpuini's
reign.[21] The same must be said for our text, precisely because of the presence of the name of Ispuini's
grandson. Therefore the situla can be dated around 810 B.C., which is approximately the transition
between the reign of Išpuini and that of Menua.[22]

Inušpua, who has not left any inscription of his own, was the heir apparent but never succeeded to the
throne, probably because he died before his father Menua. Instead a younger son of Menua, Argišti Ist,
became king (see n. 20). As at the time in which our situla was made the grandfather Išpuini was still
alive, we can assume that the grandson Inušpua was still a child.

At this point one must inquire into the meaning of ^{LÚ} *kibāru/kibarru*, referred to Inušpua. It is a word
unknown in Neo-assyrian and generally in Akkadian language, and it is impossible to connect it to any
known Urartian word.[23]

The most simple solution, theoretically, would be to recognize ^{LÚ}*k.* as a synonym of *mar'i mar'i* "grandson." K. Deller reminds me of the list of foreign synonyms for *māru* "son" in the series *šarru = malku*
I 147-159, where, however, there are no synonyms for "grandson." Deller furthermore notes, that kinship
words with determinative LÚ are very rare.

However I wonder if this word means not directly the family relationship ("grandson"), but the position
of Inušpua as "heir of the heir" Menua. In one sense, this suggestion can be conforted by the Tabriz
Kapisi inscription, quoted above, where we have all three names, father, son and grandson. In both cases
we are, perhaps, confronted with the care of Išpuini of assuring the continuity of the royal house.

The lack of any knowledge either as to place and circumstances of discovery, do not allow us to make
any assumption as to whether the situla was part of a funerary gift (perhaps from the tomb of Inušpua
himself), or whether it was part of a treasure.

---

[19]Until we have proof to the contrary, I exclude the possibility of the existence of another Inušpua, beside the grandson
of Išpuini. In the Urartian texts there are no cases of two people, one of the royal family and the other a commoner
(for ex. an official) bearing the same name.

[20]Cf. *RLA* V, p. 136, s.v. Inušpua.

[21]806 B.C. according to König, *HchI* p. 1, and Th. Beran, in H. Schmökel, *Kulturgeschichte des Alten Orient*, Stuttgart
1961, p. 609.

[22]Around 810 B.C. according to G. A. Melikišvili, *Nairi-Urartu*, Tbilisi 1954, p. 205, and B. B. Piotrovskij, *Il regno di
Van-Urartu*, Rome 1966, p. 53, 87.

[23]The Akkadian dictionaries are of no assistance: *kibarru* (CAD K 329 b) is, as suggested by K. Deller, a scribal error for
maškiru, while *kiparu* (CAD K 396 b) leads us to an Elamite milieu. Furthermore a parallel with *gibba/uru* (AHw p.
287 a) is highly dubious.

EIN MITTELASSYRISCHER BĀRI'U

Claudio Saporetti

Some middle-assyrian texts quoting the name of the same *bāri'u* are not contemporaneous. It follows that there was a tradition of names and of profession within the same family.

Als Nr. 5 seiner Mittelassyrischen Rechtsurkunden und Verwaltungstexte (I = VS NF III, Berlin 1976) hat H. Freydank den Text VAT 18004 veröffentlicht. In der Inhaltsübersicht (S. 11) beschreibt er ihn als "Verzeichnis der 'Grossen' einiger ziviler und militärischer Mannschaften und einiger Städte."[1] Unter ihnen finden sich ein Ober-Exorzist, ein Ober-Haruspex, ein Ober-Dolmetscher, ein Ober-Vogelfänger, mehrere Bezirksvorsteher und Gouverneure.

Z.3 wird ein ^{Id}UD-MU-*le-šir* GAL ^{LÚ}ḪAL^{MEŠ}, also Šamaš-šumu-lēšir *rab bāri'ē*, Ober-Haruspex, erwähnt, der natürlich an einen aus Kolophonen bekannten *bāri'u* gleichen Namens erinnert; er figuriert stets als Vater des *bāri'u* Šamaš-zēra-iddina. Die vier bislang veröffentlichten Belege sind:

ŠU $^{I\lceil d\rceil}$[U]D-NUMUN-SUM-*na* ^{LÚ}ḪAL DUMU ^{d}UD-MU-SI.SÁ ḪAL-*ma*[2]

ŠU ^{Id}UD-NUMUN-SUM-*na* DUMU ^{d}UD-MU-SI.SÁ ^{LÚ}ḪAL[3]

ŠU ^{Id}UD-NUMUN-SUM-*na* DUMU ^{d}UD-MU-SI.SÁ ḪAL[4]

ŠU ^{Id}UD-NUMUN-SUM-*na* ḪAL DUMU ^{d}UD-MU-*l*[*e-šìr* ḪAL(-*ma*)]¡[5]

Um festzustellen, ob zwischen Šamaš-šumu-lēšir VS NF III 5:3 und Šamaš-šumu-lēšir der Kolophone Personengleichheit besteht, müssen die Datierungen untersucht werden.

VS NF III 5:31 bietet das Datum ^{ITU}*ša sa-ra-a-te* U$_4$ 29 KÁM li-mu ^{Id}*Šùl-ma-nu*-MU-PA[P]. Nach einer Kollation von J. N. Postgate[6] ist auch der Eponym von TR 2021+2051:22 ^{Id}*šùl-ma-nu*-MU-PAP¡ zu lesen. Da alle mittelassyrischen Texte aus Tell Rimāḥ entweder aus der Zeit Salmanassars I. oder Tukulti-Ninurtas I. stammen,[7] sind die Datierungsmöglichkeiten bereits erheblich eingeschränkt. Nach freundlicher Mitteilung von H. Freydank erscheint der Eponym Šulmānu (Sal[mānu?]-šuma-uṣur auch in der unveröffentlichten mittelassyrischen Urkunde VAT 18007, die mit Sicherheit aus der Zeit Tukulti-Ninurtas I. stammt.

---

[1] Vgl. zu diesem Text auch H. Freydank, Altorientalische Forschungen 4 (Berlin 1976) 111ff.

[2] Assur 17344 = VAT 13798 = AfO 16, Tf. XIII; s. E. Weidner, AfO 16,210a Nr. 77.

[3] Assur 4531$^{(a)}$ = VAT 10168 = KAR 152; s. E. Weidner, AfO 16,210a/b, Nr. 78.

[4] Assur 4530 = Photo K 424/425 = A 8 = Helga Tschinkowitz, Ein Opferschautext aus dem Eponymenjahr Tiglatpilesers I., AfO 22,59-62 (Photo S.60-61); vgl. bereits E. Weidner, AfO 16,210b Nr. 80.

[5] Rm 2,101 = AfO 16, Tf. XII links; s. E. Weidner, AfO 16,210b Nr. 81 (das zu Rm 2,101 gehörige Fragment ist jedoch nicht K.250, sondern K.205; vgl. R. Borger, HKL II 381). Nach der Kopie E. Weidners ist im Patronym eher l[e-šir als S[I.SÁ zu lesen.

[6] OA 13 (1974) 71; vgl. bereits C. Saporetti, OMA I 469 und s. H. Freydank, VS NF III, S.11.

[7] C. Saporetti, Mesopotamia 8-9 (1973/74) 169f.

Die Kolophone hingegen weisen folgende Datierungen auf:

⌐ITU¬ ⌐APIN¬ ⌐ITU¬⌐Si¬-ip-p[u U$_4$ n+]2 KÁM li-⌐mu¬ I⌐x x x¬[   ]^8
[^{ITU} MN U$_4$ n KÁM l]i-mu ^{I}Be-re-e šá-kin KUR$^!$ ^{9} URU4*-DINGIR^{10}
^{ITU}DU$_6$ U$_4$ 11 KÁM li-mu $^{I\cdot GIŠ}$TUKUL-ti-IBILA-É-Š[ÁR.RA]^{11}
^{ITU}DU$_6$^{ITU}<Qar>-ra-a-tu U$_4$ 20 KÁM li-mu ^{I}TA-^{d}A-šur-ŠÀM-šu^{12}

Zwei der Datierungen weisen doppelte Monatsangabe, nach dem Nippur- und nach dem assyrischen Kalender auf; dieses Verfahren wurde mit Sicherheit vor Tiglatpileser I. nicht angewandt und ist wahrscheinlich charakteristisch für Datierungen aus der Regierungszeit dieses Königs. Damit stimmt überein, dass ein Kolophon aus dem Eponymatsjahr Tiglatpilesers I. selbst stammt. Der Eponym Ištu-Aššur-ašāmšu begegnet noch auf einem Tonkrug^{13} ^{5}^{ITU}Si-pu U$_4$ 20 KÁM li-mu ^{I}Iš-tu-Aš+šur-a-šàm-šu ^{6}DUMU ^{I}Aš+šur-ŠEŠ-SUM-na. Dieser Tonkrug enthielt Tontafeln betreffend die Tätigkeit des kakardinnu^{14} und des Ölkelterers des Aššur-Tempels; sie waren, nach Z.2 der Inschrift, dem Ezbu-lēšir, rab ginā'e des Aššur-Tempels, unterstellt, der in Z.3-4 als Untergebener (ÌR, urdu) des Königs Tiglatpilesers bezeichnet wird. Somit ist auch der Ninua-Text Rm 2,101 in die Zeit dieses Herrschers zu datieren. Möglicherweise ist der rab ginā'e Ezbu-lēšir identisch mit einem Träger gleichen Namens, der in dem unveröffentlichen Text Assur 18773 Rs 8^{15} erwähnt wird, dessen Eponym Mudammiq-Bēl ebenfalls der Regierungszeit Tiglatpilesers I. zurechnen ist.^{16}

Der Eponym Berê wird von E. Weidner^{17} ebenfalls in die Zeit Tiglatpilesers angesetzt; ausser KAR 152 lassen sich allerdings nur Assur 23128 (unveröffentlicht) und "ein anderer Assur-Text (Fund-Nummer nicht mehr festzustellen)" nachweisen.

Der bāri'u Šamaš-šumu-lēšir, der Vater des bāri'u Šamaš-zēra-iddina, der Kolophone gehöhrt also in die Zeit des Tiglatpilesers I. oder höchstens eine Generation vor dessen Regierungszeit. Er kann demnach nicht personengleich mit dem rab bāri'e Šamaš-šumu-lēšir des Verzeichnisses der 'Grossen' sein, das nach der Regierungszeit Tukulti-Ninurtas I. zu datieren ist.

Die Minimaldistanz, vom Tod des Tukulti-Ninurta I. (1208 v. Chr.) bis zur Akzession des Tiglatpilesers I. (1115 v. Chr.) begrägt 93 Jahre, die sich unter der Annahme, dass Šamaš-šumu-lēšir, der Vater des Šamaš-zēra-iddina die Inthronisation dieses Königs nicht mehr erlebt hätte, noch verringern würden. In diese Zeitspanne können eigentlich kaum mehr als drei Schreiber- bzw. bāri'u-Generationen eingefügt werden. Es wäre demnach denkbar, dass folgende Genealogie vorläge:

NN$_1$ (rab bāri'é)
Šamaš-šumu-lēšir rab bāri'ē   Zeit Tukulti-Ninurtas I.
NN$_2$ (bāri'u)

---

^{8}Assur 17344 = VAT 13798 = AfO 16, Tf. XIII; s. H. Hunger, Kolophone, Nr. 46 (B).

^{9}Autographie ŠE; Kollation E. Weidner, AfO 16,210a Nr. 78.

^{10}Assur 4531$^{(a)}$ = VAT 10168 = KAR 152; s. H. Hunger, Kolophone, Nr. 46 (C).

^{11}Assur 4530 = Photo K 425 = A 8 = AfO 22,61. Hinsichtlich der Lesung des Monatsnamens folgen wir H. Tschinkowitz, AfO 22,59a (11. Tešrit); das Zeichen DUL oder DU$_6$ ist auf dem Photo nicht ganz eindeutig.

^{12}Rm 2,101 = AfO 16, Tf. XII links; s. H. Hunger, Kolophone, Nr. 46 (A).

^{13}Assur 18766 = VA 5035. Die Aufschrift ist in Transkription mitgeteilt von E. Weidner, AfO 10,28 Anm.213.

^{14}Zu diesem, speziell aus mittel- und neuassyrischen Texten für den Aššur-Tempel nachzuweisenden Beruf vgl. E. Weidner, AfO 10,18 Anm. 127.

^{15}Vgl. E. Weidner, AfO 16,215b Nr. 28. Die Annahme, es handle sich bei diesem Ezbu-lēšir um einen Eponym (OMA I 369 sub Pirḫu-lēšir) ist irrig.

^{16}E. Weidner, AfO 13,315b und AfO 16,215b Nr. 28.

^{17}AfO 13,313b und AfO 16,215a Nr. 19.

Šamaš-šumu-lēšir   *bāri'u*
Šamaš-zera-iddina   *bāri'u*   Zeit Tiglatpilesers I.

Da das theophore Element Šamaš eine Konstante in der Namengebung dieser supponierten Familie zu sein scheint—wen überrascht es, den Namen des *bēl bīri* im Onomastikon einer *bāri'u*-Familie anzutreffen?—, darf man, mit allem Vorbehalt, folgern, dass auch NN_1 und NN_2 mit dem Namen des Sonnengottes begannen.

Auf der Suche nach einem Kandidaten für NN_2 stösst man auf [Id]UD-*na-di-in-aḫ-ḫe* DUMU [d]UD-MU-[, den Schreiber von Assur 19129 = VAT 9600 = KAR 447 Rs 8, einer Sammlung von Opferschau-Omina. Dem gleichen Schreiber verdanken wir einen weiteren Text derselben Gattung, VAT 10751 = KAR 454 (Assur-Nummer nicht mehr festzustellen).[18]   Beide Stücke hält E. Weidner[19] entweder als Importstücke im Original oder danach angefertigte Abschriften, "bei denen die babylonischen Schriftzeichen mit assyrischen Schriftzeichen untermischt sind."   Wegen der Häufigkeit der Šamaš-Namen in diesen beiden Kolophonen muss man nicht gleich an deren Herkunft aus Sippar denken;[20] ihre Profession (*bāri'u*) erklärt das theophore Element ihrer Namen hinlänglich.   Falls wir also in KAR 447 Rs 8 das Patronym zu [d]UD-MU-[*le-šir*] bzw. [d]UD-MU-[SI.SÁ] ergänzen dürfen, würde dies bedeuten, dass der ältere Šamaš-šumu-lēšir und sein Sohn Šamaš-nādin-aḫḫē bestimmte, von Tukulti-Ninurta I. in Babylon erbeutete Omentexte rezipiert und eine assyrische Tradition begründet hätten.

Zugleich könnte man dieser Genealogie ein schönes Beispiel für die Papponymie (Enkel nach dem Grossvater benannt) entnehmen.   Abschliessend sei der hypothetische Charakter dieser genealogischen Studie noch einmal ausdrücklich unterstrichen; die Rekonstruktion der mittelassyrischen Schreiberfamilien ist jedoch ein wichtiges prosopographisches Desiderat.

(Heidelberg, Sept. 1978)

---

[18]E. Weidner, AfO 16,200b x, p) und u); H. Hunger, Kolophone, Nr. 70 und Nr. 69.
[19]AfO 16,199.
[20]AfO 16,210.